Embracing the Future: How Space Organizations are Integrating Additive Manufacturing Technologies

Sunny Roy

Copyright © [2023]

Title: Embracing the Future: How Space Organizations are Integrating Additive Manufacturing Technologies
Author's: Sunny Roy

All rights reserved. No part of this publication may be reproduced, stored in a retrieval system, or transmitted in any form or by any means, electronic, mechanical, photocopying, recording, or otherwise, without the prior written permission of the publisher or author, except in the case of brief quotations embodied in critical reviews and certain other non-commercial uses permitted by copyright law.

This book was printed and published by [**Publisher's: Sunny Roy**] in [2023]

ISBN:

Contents

1 **Introduction** 1
   1.1 Research Context and Motivations 1
   1.2 INESC TEC and CESE 2
   1.3 Objectives 3
   1.4 Methodology 3
   1.5 Outline of the book 4

2 **Literature Review** 5
   2.1 Additive Manufacturing 5
      2.1.1 Technologies and Materials 7
      2.1.2 Design Optimisation 12
      2.1.3 Opportunities in the Space Sector 13
   2.2 Technology Adoption in Organisations 15
      2.2.1 The Diffusion of Innovation Theory 17
      2.2.2 The Technology-Organisation-Environment (TOE) Framework 20

3 **Research Method** 23
   3.1 Research Design 23
   3.2 Data Collection 24
   3.3 Data Analysis 29

4 **Results** 31
   4.1 Opportunities for AM in the Space Sector 31
   4.2 Technology 33
      4.2.1 Relative Advantage 33
      4.2.2 Compatibility 34
      4.2.3 Trialability 34
      4.2.4 Observability 35
   4.3 Organisation 35
      4.3.1 Adoption Cost 35
      4.3.2 Organisational Readiness 36
      4.3.3 Organisational Innovativeness 36
   4.4 Environment 36
      4.4.1 Space Agencies' Support 36
      4.4.2 Space Agencies' Pressure 37

5 **Discussion** 39

6 Conclusion **43**
    6.1   Future Work 44

Chapter 1

Introduction

The present document was written within the scope of the curricular unit "book", which is part of the curriculum of the 2nd and final year of the Masters in Mechanical Engineering at FEUP (Faculty of Engineering of the University of Porto). This book was written at INESC TEC, a research association dedicated to scientific research and technological development. In particular, the work was developed in the Enterprise Systems Engineering Centre (CESE).

1.1 Research Context and Motivations

In a world of fast-evolving technology, space activities contribute to innovation and have an impact on every-day life. Some of these activities include space exploration for scientific purposes, development of communication and earth-observation satellites, permanent human presence on the International Space Station (ISS) and even planetary settlement (Blakey-Milner et al., 2021).

Traditionally, most space activities were carried out by government agencies, and, as a result, long-term and disruptive change was limited and dependant on the technological recommendations of the space agencies (Summerer, 2012). However, a new era is emerging in the space sector, known as *New Space*, and the building, launching, and operating of spacecraft is also being explored by new entrants in this industry (Denis et al., 2020). New Space has been defined as "a disruptive sectorial dynamic featuring various end-to-end efficiency-driven concepts leading the space sector towards a more business- and service-oriented place" (Vernile, 2018). This new era is prompting the investigation and development of innovative technologies for space, as well as the adoption and integration of previously existing technology.

Space activities are important innovation triggers across multiple sectors, that is, technology developed for space finds use in other sectors (spin-off effect), and the opposite can happen as well, where technology that wasn't developed for space is applied to space applications (spin-in effect) (Summerer, 2012). The latter applies to Additive Manufacturing (AM), also known as 3D printing, a manufacturing process that was developed in the 1980s to create objects, mainly prototypes, quickly and efficiently in industrial settings. With technological improvements throughout the years, it has become a promising innovation for a variety of industries, including biomedical, automotive, aerospace and space. In fact, the European Space Agency (ESA) has considered AM technologies to be "important contributors for an industrial revolution of space" (ESA, 2016). Being a manufacturing process, AM's potential for the space sector currently lies mainly in the optimisation of the design of different space components, resulting in less material usage, as well as in the field of in-space manufacturing, which is still in an early stage of development (Zocca et al., 2022).

Through numerous efforts from AM developers and academic researchers, more and more companies have begun using this process to take advantage of its qualities, such as the freedom of design it offers and consequent ability to manufacture geometrically complex objects (Huang et al., 2015). However, technical limitations, such as missing quality standards, organisational aspects, like the lack of qualified personnel, and external sectorial pressures are hindering the wide adoption of AM. All things considered, it becomes relevant to study AM in an organisational context, to identify what affects the adoption of this innovation within the space sector. Actually, the evaluation of the factors that influence the adoption of AM has been considered as a research opportunity in the field (Steenhuis and Pretorius, 2017).

1.2 INESC TEC and CESE

This book was developed at INESC TEC, a research association, with different locations in the north of Portugal, including Porto, where this project was developed. INESC TEC is a private non-profit association dedicated to scientific research, technology development, knowledge transfer, advanced consulting and training, as well as pre-incubation of technological start-ups. INESC TEC bridges universities, enterprises, public administration and society by employing results from investigation in technology transfer projects that society can benefit from. (INESC TEC, 2022b).

The organisational structure of INESC TEC contains research centres based on different fields of studies. One of these centres is CESE, the Engineering and Enterprise Centre, where this book was carried out. CESE's mission is to advance the scientific knowledge in enterprise systems engineering, and generating innovative services for industrial organisations. The areas of focus are Production Systems Design, Planning and Management, Collaborative Platforms, Supply Chain Strategy, Industry-level Intelligent Production, Transportation and Logistics and Technology Management in Industry (INESC TEC, 2022a). Figure 1.1 shows the logo of INESC TEC.

Figure 1.1: INESC TEC Logo. Source: INESC TEC (2017)

The project which originated this book is called *NewSat*, a Flagship Project of MIT Portugal which aims to develop and ground test a nanosatellite that will contribute to characterise Earth's upper atmosphere (ionosphere). The data obtained will be used to calculate the electrical properties of the ionosphere, and, consequently, allow for a better assessment of aerosol behaviour and cloud formation, crucial for the development of Earth climate models, particularly in a climate change context. The structure, sensors and thrusters developed for NewSat are to be achieved using additive manufacturing technology (MIT Portugal, 2020).

1.3 Objectives

This book aims to analyse the main adoption factors that influence the use of additive manufacturing by space organisations. While the literature on the technological aspects of AM is extensive and informative, potential applications and concrete adoption factors haven't yet been empirically revised, especially for the space sector. Hence, the main questions that drive the realisation of this book are:

- What are the main technological benefits of AM to the space sector?

- What are the main space-related applications that AM can be used for?

- What influences the adoption of innovation in organisations, and how can this be applied to AM in the space sector?

Keeping these questions in mind, as well as the research opportunity that this under-explored field represents, this book aims to fill a research gap, while also contributing to a growing body of literature in the subject of additive manufacturing applied to the space sector.

1.4 Methodology

To fulfil the objective of this book, two concepts were used, as theoretical basis for results' analysis: the Diffusion of Innovations Theory and Technology Organisation and Environment Framework. For this exploratory work, which discusses a topic that hasn't been widely studied yet, a qualitative study was deemed appropriate, as it enables a deeper analysis of the factors that affect the adoption of AM by space organisations. Semi-structured interviews were conducted with ten experts, representing private companies, the European Space Agency, and a research institute. The interviews were recorded, and later transcribed and examined through MAXQDA, a data analysis software that permits the categorisation of excerpts from the interviews in topics of interest. The categories used for data analysis followed the adoption factors proposed by the TOE framework and the DOI theory, both adapted to better suit the theme of this book.

1.5 Outline of the book

The remaining sections of this book are organised as follows:

- **Chapter 2:** theoretical background review of relevant topics to the theme
- **Chapter 3:** methodology followed in this study, to obtain significant data
- **Chapter 4:** results obtained from the investigation
- **Chapter 5:** discussion on these results, and how they relate to the theoretical background
- **Chapter 6:** the final chapter, where conclusions are drawn and future work is suggested

Chapter 2

Literature Review

This section provides a theoretical background on concepts related to the dissertation's theme. Section 2.1 provides an overview of the additive manufacturing process, including the different technologies that exist and the materials appropriate for space applications, the design optimisation opportunities for AM and the current trends in the use of AM in the space sector. Section 2.2 explores the theoretical contexts that describe the decision processes of organisations and individuals when pondering the adoption and implementation a technological innovation.

2.1 Additive Manufacturing

Additive Manufacturing is defined by the American Society for Testing and Materials (ASTM) as "the process of joining materials to make objects from 3D model data, usually layer upon layer, as opposed to subtractive manufacturing technologies" (ASTM, 2012). In other words, AM consists of making parts by adding material in layers along the z-axis, and each layer is a thin cross section of the part derived from the original Computer Aided Design (CAD) model. In general, 6 steps are necessary to build a 3D printed part, from the CAD model to the final application (Ian Gibson and Stucker, 2015) (All3DP, 2021) (Kumbhar and Mulay, 2018):

1. **CAD model:** all AM parts start with a software model (CAD) that fully describes the object's geometry, as a 3D representation, like the one shown in Figure 2.1, on the left, and in Figure 2.2, on top.
2. **STL file conversion:** .stl is a file format that is accepted by nearly all 3D printers. It represents the surface geometry without colour or texture. The representation of an STL file is in Figure 2.1, on the right, and in Figure 2.2, on the bottom. The printer then converts this digital model into printing instructions, which consist of hundreds, or thousands of horizontal layers which will be placed over one another until the final shape is achieved.

Figure 2.1: CAD model (left) and STL file (right). Source: Ian Gibson and Stucker (2015)

Figure 2.2: CAD (top) and STL (bottom) details. Source: Additive Manufacturing India (2018)

3. **Machine Setup and Building:** machine setup refers to system settings that must be set prior to building, including material constraints, energy source and timings. Building is highly automated and heavily dependent on the process category to be used. The various process categories will be described in Subsection 2.1.1. Examples of 3D printing machines are presented in Figures 2.3 and 2.4, being the latter the 3D printer in the International Space Station (ISS).

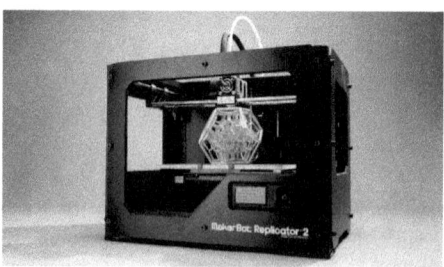

Figure 2.3: 3D Printer. Source: 3D Beginners (2022)

2.1 Additive Manufacturing

Figure 2.4: ISS 3D Printer. Source: NASA (2014)

4. **Removal:** once the part is complete, it must be safely removed from the printer's chamber.
5. **Post-Processing:** parts made using AM often exhibit poor surface quality and, as such, post-processing is usually necessary, like machining, painting or performing abrasion.
6. **Ready for use:** after the process is complete, the part is finished and ready to be used or assembled with other elements. Figure 2.5 shows a final 3D printed part: a bracket used in an ESA's Ariane launcher.

Figure 2.5: 3D printed part. Source: ESA (2019)

2.1.1 Technologies and Materials

Additive Manufacturing is classified into seven processes, which are displayed in Table 2.1. Each process category is characterised by a singular machine architecture and, consequently, similar materials' transformation physics. Within each category are corresponding technologies, which differ mainly in the heating source that is used (Ian Gibson and Stucker, 2015).

Table 2.1: Additive Manufacturing Technologies, adapted from Huang et al. (2015), Ian Gibson and Stucker (2015) and Calignano et al. (2017)

Process Categories	Technologies	Description	Material
Vat Photopolymerisation (VPP)	SLA	Uses a vat (or container) of liquid photopolymer resin, out of which the model is constructed layer by layer, on a plate that moves downwards, whilst each layer is being curated by a UV light.	UV curable resins
Powder Bed Fusion (PBF)	DMLS, SLS, SLM, SHS, EBM	The material is in powder form in a plate, and an energy source moves through it, to fuse the material into the desired form. This energy source can be a laser, this is the case for DMLS, SLS and SLM, a high-power electron beam, for EBM, or even a heated print-head, for SHS.	Mostly metals, but Thermoplastics can be used with SLS
Material Extrusion (MEX)	FDM or FFF	The raw material is heated to a molten state, and then extruded through the nozzle of the 3D printer, while creating the pattern.	Thermoplastics, waxes
Material Jetting (MJT)	MJT	Objects are created by deposition of material in a continuous stream, or drops, onto a surface, where it solidifies. The model is built layer by layer.	UV curable resins, waxes
Binder Jetting (BJT)	3DP	The powder is processed with a liquid adhesive, which binds the powder layers together. The object is built as the platform is lowered, while the print head moves horizontally.	Composites, polymers, ceramics, metals
Sheet Lamination (SHL)	LOM	Sheets of material are bonded together to form a part.	Paper, metals and thermoplastics
Directed Energy Deposition (DED)	LMD/LENS, EBAM	DED processes use raw materials in the form of powder or wire, and deposit the material to desired shape, while simultaneously melting it, with an energy source.	Metals

2.1 Additive Manufacturing

Table 2.1 shows that certain materials are more appropriate for certain processes and/or technologies than others. So, the material and technology are chosen according to the application of the final part. For space applications, products must comply with high reliability requirements, due to the extreme conditions in rocket launch and satellite operations (Borgue et al., 2018). These extreme conditions refer mainly to the launching environment and the in-orbit permanence. The first one is characterised by extreme temperatures, significantly high vibrations, acoustic and shock levels, thermal fluxes, lightning and potential bird strikes, whereas the latter refers to the space environment, where all the external loads and the atmosphere disappear and spacecraft materials are exposed to vacuum (Ghidini, 2018).

The hostile in-orbit environment comes with three main issues that spacecraft materials must endure, particularly in Low Earth Orbit (between 200 km and 700 km in altitude), where most space activities are conducted (for example, the ISS is in LEO, as well as most satellites). They are the **vacuum**, the **extreme temperature variation**, and the high concentration of **atomic oxygen**. Resistance to the negative effects of vacuum in space can be determined by whether a material exhibits outgassing [1] or not. So, materials that are exposed to the space environment, should exhibit low outgassing. This is considered one of the most crucial challenges concerning the choice of materials for spacecraft (Edward Silverman, 1995). The principal repercussions of outgassing are contamination of surfaces, loss of dimensional stability, which cause negative effects on material qualities, being these effects become more prominent at higher temperatures (Grossman and Gouzman, 2003). At LEO, temperatures generally range from -100°C to +100°C. Such temperature variation causes thermal stresses in materials which can cause cracking of parts, spalling of the surface treatment layers and damaging of the electronic assemblies. To prevent this, the coefficient of thermal expansion (CTE), a property that represents the rate at which a material expands with increase in temperature, must be very low, to accommodate the extreme temperatures (Toropova and Steeves, 2015). The final main threat for materials in LEO is the exposure to a flux of atomic oxygen. The leading effect of atomic oxygen is the erosion of materials (both metallic and polymeric) and coatings, and their flaking-off with considerable risk of contamination and degradation of the functionality of the layer (Ghidini, 2018).

To this day, metallic materials have are preferred for space applications, especially in structural functions. Metals generally offer great mechanical properties, like stiffness and tensile strength, important for the launching phase, as well as low outgassing levels. Regarding AM metallic parts for space, this manufacturing process has been gaining importance in the industry, to produce components for launch vehicles and satellites (Blakey-Milner et al., 2021). In 2011, the first AM spacecraft structures were launched on the Juno mission to Jupiter. The components are a set of eight brackets one of which is shown in Figure 2.6 (NASA Press Kit, 2016).

---

[1] Outgassing is the release of gaseous species from materials under high vacuum conditions.

Figure 2.6: 3D printed titanium brackets, before (left) and after (right) machining. Source: Peter Zelinski (2016)

The main process categories for the fabrication of metal components are DED and PBF. While nearly all the applications of AM that fabricate metal parts require some post processing, heat treatment and finishing, PBF AM processes may be considered near-net shape. The primary heat sources for these processes are laser and electron beam (EB). The commonly used materials for metal AM are stainless steel, nickel-base superalloys, titanium alloys, tool steels and aluminium alloys (DebRoy et al., 2018). Due to the mass saving aspect inherent to spacecraft manufacturing, titanium alloys are interesting for this application. Titanium's low density, high strength and long-term chemical compatibility with fuel are properties that prompt its use in space missions (Peters et al., 2003). The most extensively investigated titanium alloy is Ti-6Al-4V, a material that allows for complex, low production volume of titanium parts (Frazier, 2014). The use of this alloy for space applications has been especially with the DED process and EBAM technology for larger components and repairs, and with the PBF process and SLM and EBM technologies for smaller but more complex parts (Wang et al., 2016) (Sames et al., 2016). This material offers high specific strength, fracture toughness, fatigue resistance and excellent corrosion resistance (Lütjering and Williams, 2007). However, one of the major limitations of titanium alloys is their high cost, which can be overcome with the development of low-cost technologies for the recycling of Ti alloys (Anil Kumar and Prasad, 2021).

The most usual building materials for AM technologies, across all sectors, are thermoplastic and thermoset polymers. AM's evolution in the industry has been inextricably linked to advances in the understanding of how these polymers are processed. Almost all AM technologies can use thermoplastics or thermoset polymers as building materials and they generally don't require post processing (Ligon et al., 2017). The applications of polymeric materials in the space sector are, however, limited, according to ESA standards (European Cooperation for Space Standardisation, 2004).

Thermoplastics find multiple uses in spacecraft, including electrical insulators, gaskets and small mechanical parts (Kelly, 2012). The class of thermoplastics contains numerous materials, among which is Polyetheretherketone (PEEK), a semi-crystalline high-performance thermoplastic polymer. PEEK is suitable in many engineering applications, including medical instruments and automotive engine parts. It has potential applicability in the space sector, doesn't exhibit

2.1 Additive Manufacturing

outgassing and possesses great chemical resistance, mechanical strength and dimensional stability (Rinaldi et al., 2018). Additionally, due to its excellent strength-to-weight ratio, PEEK can even substitute metals in some applications, including spare parts for out-of-the-earth manufacturing (Zanjanijam et al., 2020). Figure 2.7 shows a 3D printed nanosatellite structure (a nanosatellite is a satellite that weighs between 1 and 10 kg), made as a proof-of-concept to demonstrate the mechanical properties of this material in space applications. It uses PEEK as the material and FDM as the technology.

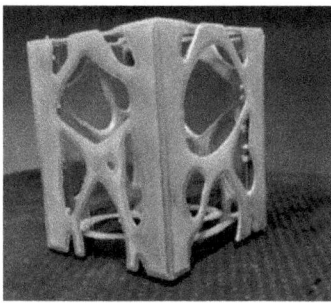

Figure 2.7: 3D Printed PEEK nanosatellite model. Source: Rinaldi et al. (2021)

In general, thermoset polymers aren't the most adequate for space use, maily because they exhibit outgassing, which doesn't degrade material properties, but can lead to contamination (Wu and Koo, 2022). Furthermore, the thermal expansion can be quite large in these polymers, leading to cracks and consequent degradation of properties. Also, atomic oxygen has a negative effect on thermosets, leading to environment contamination. As such, thermoset polymers are mainly used as the matrix for fibre reinforced polymers, another class of materials introduced in the following paragraph (European Cooperation for Space Standardisation, 2004).

Fibre Reinforced Polymers (FRP), also known as composites, are materials that result from an amalgamation of two or more constituents, one of which is present in the matrix (for example, a thermoset polymer), and another one that is in fibre form (for example, carbon fibre) (Rajak et al., 2019). Composite materials may be used to replace traditional materials with the goal of reducing weight and improve stiffness and strength or, in other cases, the composite product has intrinsically unique products that couldn't be attained with other materials (Radford, 2018). Applications for FRP in structural and semi-structural applications include honeycomb pannels (structures used with the goal of mass reduction, such as the one shown in Figure 2.8), antennas, trays, spacecraft skins, among others (European Cooperation for Space Standardisation, 2004). Additive manufacturing of FRP is an emerging and trending field with the potential to produce parts with improved mechanical properties, compared to un-reinforced polymers. To be processed by AM, FRP materials must meet certain characteristics, including good fibre-to-matrix bonding, fibre homogeneity, fibre alignment, good inter-layer bonding and minimal porosity (Goh et al., 2019). The technologies that have been used with composites are LOM, SLS and FFF , and, even though the results are promising, they aren't as good as the ones obtained with conventionally manufactured composite objects (Ngo et al., 2018). This brings up new possibilities for AM technologies to improve the mechanical properties of FRP materials through material development and process improvement (Goh et al., 2019).

Figure 2.8: High-performance carbon fiber honeycomb for special applications. Source: Rinaldi et al. (2021)

Alongside the choice of material and technology, the design of parts for AM plays a key role in ensuring that the final part performs well and that the process is being explored to its full potential. Because of the ability for creating extremely complex geometrical shapes using AM, re-imagining the design process becomes an interesting and necessary task. Without the geometrical limitations imposed by conventional manufacturing processes, AM makes it possible to create structurally optimised structures, which can be adapted to specific functions. Section 2.1.3 showcases the design aspect of AM, current trends, and why it's important.

2.1.2 Design Optimisation

The lack of development of design tools, rules, processes and methodologies specific for AM has been cited as one of its main technical challenges, and it is said to be limiting the overall adoption of AM in the industry (Platform, 2015). Designing parts for AM aims to explore the full capacities of this manufacturing process, by producing structures with complex geometries, low mass and potentially multiple functionalities (Gaudenzi et al., 2018). Actually, the demand for highly complex products made with AM has prompted research in the introduction of multiple functionalities into a single object, like mechanical, thermal and optical (Han and Lee, 2020).

One method for achieving optimal lightweight structures is Topology Optimisation (TO), defined as a mathematical design method used to optimise material usage in structural applications, considering a set of external loads and constraints (Blakey-Milner et al., 2021). It is based

2.1 Additive Manufacturing

on simulations and iterative optimisations, utilising a finite element method to improve design performance. It was introduced by Bendsøe and Kikuchi (1988) and answers the fundamental engineering question: "How should material be placed, within a given domain, in order to obtain the best structural performance?" (Sigmund and Maute, 2013). During the design process, a topology optimisation software can be used to place material in response to the loads carried by the item. Because of the comparable design rules to biological evolution, the final objects can look differently from traditionally designed ones and frequently appear strangely organic. An example of the use of TO for space applications is in satellites' brackets, that serve as a link between the body of the satellite and the reflectors. By combining topology optimisation techniques with AM technologies, new brackets were produced for Eurostar E3000 (Airbus Defence and Space) telecommunications satellites manufactured with aluminium alloy. (Calignano et al., 2017). The resulting brackets are shown in Figure 2.9.

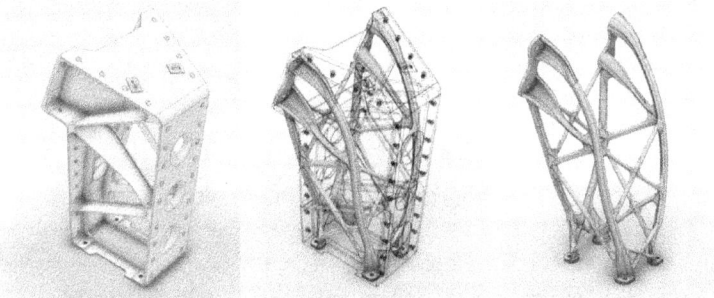

Figure 2.9: Model of optimised satellite brackets using TO. Source: Airbus Defence and Space (2022)

Having discussed the process of producing parts using AM, from the choice of materials to the optimisation of design, Subsection 2.1.3 will focus on AM applied to the space sector, and the main trends found in literature about this subject.

2.1.3 Opportunities in the Space Sector

In the era of New Space, where new entrants in the industry are looking for ways to reduce launching costs and making access to space easy and affordable, the miniaturisation of spacecraft is verified. Naturally, smaller and lighter structures are cheaper to launch, since the cost of space launches is directly related to the mass of spacecraft. Indeed, the launching of 1kg to space costs thousands of dollars (Toorian et al., 2008). This is the reason why mass reduction is so crucial in satellite manufacturing, and where much of the potential of AM for this industry lies. In sum, space components must be as lightweight as possible, reducing the launching costs and increasing the number of small satellites per payload, and they must perform well under the harsh conditions of the space environment (Calignano et al., 2017). AM technologies constitute an interesting option for the manufacturing of small satellites, since they enable the construction of a better and more flexible product, at less cost and in a shorter time, as well as the possibility for customisation. Among this class of small satellites are CubeSats, as shown in 2.10, firstly developed for academic and research purposes, but currently used for commercial purposes as well. Cubesats are built in standard dimensions, or Units, "U", of 10cm x 10 cm x 10 cm, and with less than 1.33kg, and they can be 1U, 2U, 3U or 6U (NASA, 2018). They are also characterised by the use of Commercial Off The Shelf (COTS) components, further emphasising the cost reduction these satellites represent (NASA, 2018).

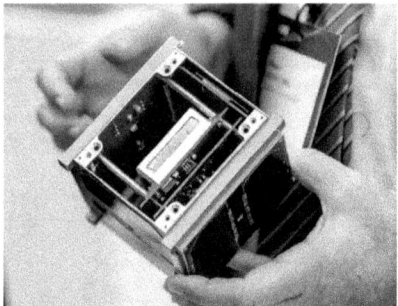

Figure 2.10: CubeSat. Source: Tech2 (2022)

With the development of small satellites comes the constitution of large constellations of these satellites operated by private companies and space agencies. These large constellations of small satellites provide global coverage, allowing for better communications services worldwide, as well as benefits for Earth and Space observation, allowing near real-time measurements, monitoring and surveillance (Curzi et al., 2020). However, they are complex systems, and require substantial effort in designing, manufacturing, launching and maintaining (Denis et al., 2020). To keep up with the commercial demand of a large number of spacecraft in a short amount of time, a paradigm shift is required in the way that satellites are manufactured. Additive Manufacturing technologies, with their potential for customisation, often necessary in spacecraft components' manufacturing, constitute an appealing option to be addressed. (Gaudenzi et al., 2018). The potential of AM, often referred to as a process for customised serial production, in this industry, lies mainly in the possibility to obtain lightweight and complex structures. Also, the possibility to reduce the number of parts through high levels of multifunctional integration, is an interesting application for AM. The literature on using AM for CubeSat structures reveals success cases, as AM provided significant mass reduction, reduction of the number of components and, consequently, a decrease in potential failure location (Rinaldi et al., 2018) (Ghidini, 2018).

During space missions, which often take last for long periods of time and travel long distances, it's challenging to anticipate and prepare for all possible scenarios of machine failures, accidents, among other challenges that can occur. Thus, the field of "in-space" manufacturing is gaining importance and AM is at the forefront of it (Zocca et al., 2022). Furthermore, with human exploration of the Moon and Mars, that is, planetary settlement missions, local resources, like Moon and Mars regolith (the planet soil) are being used for the manufacturing of these structures and repair components (Ghidini, 2018). The use of AM technologies in space comes with its own challenges, being the main one the effect of zero-gravity. In the absence of gravity, surface tension forces become important determinants of system behaviour, potentially affecting the mechanical and functional integrity of the finished part. Additionally, an entirely new approach to positioning for part production is required, and additional caution with floating debris, which may damage the machine, is necessary (National Research Council, 2014). The use of AM in space missions has been tested for the production of replacement components, repair tools and even biological tissue (Makaya et al., 2022). Also, an ESA study demonstrated the use of AM for planetary permanent settlement, where a 1.5 tonne Moon base segment using regolith was successfully fabricated using AM, shown in Figure 2.11.

Figure 2.11: Moonbase segment made of regolith. Source: ESA (2017)

In sum, the transition of AM from technique used for rapid prototyping and tooling to the production of final parts is complex, and not only related to technical aspects of AM, as there are plenty other factors which impact an organisation's adoption of a new technology. Section 2.2 will explore with these factors, introducing theoretical frameworks.

2.2 Technology Adoption in Organisations

The subject of innovations, their impact on economic development and society has been a topic of interest among academics for decades. So, naturally, several definitions of innovation have emerged. Rogers and Shoemaker (1971) define it as "an idea, practice, or object perceived as new by the individual". In a more recent content analysis study, with the specific goal of proposing an integrative definition of innovation, Baregheh et al. (2009) define it as "the multi-stage process whereby organisations transform ideas into new/improved products, services or processes, in order to advance, compete and differentiate themselves successfully in their marketplace". When it comes to adopting and integrating innovation in an organisational context, two opposite concepts exist: **closed innovation**, where companies generate their own innovative ideas, later developing, financing and distributing them on their own and **open innovation**, where companies and universities expand their relationship networks, using internal and external knowledge sources to develop their R&D activities (Chesbrough, 2006). The basic premise of open innovation is to broaden it by integrating external players into the innovative process, such as research institutes, suppliers and customers (Eelko K.R.E. Huizingh, 2011). Innovation, as the driver for socio-economic development is guided by technological advances, which ensure firms' competitive advantage in the marketplace. The process of integrating innovative technologies requires management strategies and often changes in the organisational structure, in order to successfully capture the potential benefits of the venture (Nelson and Winter, 2002).

To evaluate the maturity of a technological innovation, and consequent adequacy for commercialisation, NASA introduced the concept of Technology Readiness Levels (TRL), a metric has been used widely, particularly in space technology, for which it was developed (Mankins, 1995). This metric allows to provide personnel with an awareness of how much development a certain technology requires before being commercially utilised. The TRL scale is divided in nine levels:

- **TRL 1:** basic principles are observed and reported. In this stage, scientific research is gathered on the topic, and the technology's properties are evaluated.
- **TRL 2:** technology concept and/or application is formulated. After research, practical applications can be developed.
- **TRL 3:** analytical and experimental proof of concept. Experimental studies are performed, to physically validate the analytical predictions of separate components.
- **TRL 4:** component and/or system validation in laboratory environment. The different components are tested together to evaluate functionality.
- **TRL 5:** laboratory scale, system validation in relevant environment. Simulation of the environment is made, to test the prototype in.
- **TRL 6:** engineering/pilot-scale, prototypical system validation in relevant environment. More strict tests are performed, in the equipment's final form, featuring all components.
- **TRL 7:** full-scale, similar (prototypical) system demonstrated in relevant environment. The finished prototype is tested in the environment it's supposed to be used in.
- **TRL 8:** system completed and qualified through test and demonstration. The technology has been proven to work in its final form and under expected conditions.
- **TRL 9:** actual system operated over the full range of expected conditions. The technology is in its final form, and has been operated under the full range of operating conditions.

The TRL can be used as a guide for technology maturation, a process that begins with basic and general research into new technologies and concepts and ends with system launch and operations

2.2 Technology Adoption in Organisations 17

(Mankins, 1995). While AM systems and platforms are mature and have a high TRL, the TRL of AM parts configured for spaceflight varies according to the material, the configuration of the actual part, the material's manufacturing process, the postprocessing of the manufactured part, the testing and qualification process, and many other factors. For example, the bulk structural characteristics of nylon manufactured with an FFF technique will differ from nylon fabricated with an SLS system. That is, a TRL could be assigned to a component made with a given manufacturing technique and material (NASA, 2021).

In Sections 2.2.1 and 2.2.2, the theoretical background about technology adoption will be presented. To understand the factors that drive the adoption of innovation and how this process unravels, at the organisational level, theories about technology adoption are valuable .

2.2.1 The Diffusion of Innovation Theory

The Diffusion of Innovation theory (DOI) was firstly proposed by E.M. Rogers in 1962. It consists of a body of knowledge built around empirical work that demonstrated a consistent pattern in the adoption of new ideas over time by people and/or organisations in a social system (Greenhalgh et al., 2004). Prior to adoption, people go through a decision process, defined by Rogers (1995) as "a series of actions and choices over time through which an individual or an organisation evaluates a new idea and decides whether or not to incorporate the new idea into ongoing practice". This process is divided into five stages, which happen sequentially and culminate in a definitive decision to use the innovation. The stages are shown in Figure 2.12 and further described below.

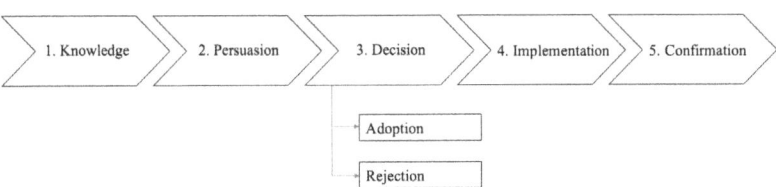

Figure 2.12: Innovation Adoption Stages. Adapted from: Rogers (1995)

1. **Knowledge:** occurs when the decision-making unit becomes aware of the innovation's existence and seeks information about how it functions. In an organisational context, it seems that the presence of an innovation will prompt its adoption, because it will likely match with an existing organisational problem. Consequently, organisations are routinely looking for innovations.

2. **Persuasion:** occurs when the decision-making unit forms a favourable or unfavourable opinion towards the innovation. In this stage, it is critical that the innovation is perceived as useful, so that the potential user decides to adopt it. However, it is important to note that

a favourable attitude towards innovation doesn't always lead to its adoption, and the same happens with an unfavourable attitude and an innovation's rejection. In sum, the Persuasion stage is where organisations haven't implemented the innovation yet, but are familiar with it, interested and willing to adopt it, or not, and are familiar with it.

3. **Decision:** occurs when the decision-making unit engages in activities that lead to a choice to adopt or reject the innovation. This is a stage of experimentation, where the decision-making unit hasn't fully committed to it yet, but have actively made a choice about whether or not to adopt it.

4. **Implementation:** occurs when the decision-making unit puts an innovation to use, even if for limited applications only. In organisations, problems with implementation may appear, especially if decision making unit is often not composed of the same people as the ones who are effectively going to use the innovation.

5. **Confirmation:** occurs when the decision-making unit seeks reinforcement of a decision that's already been made, but it's still willing to reverse said decision, if new intervening factors appear. In a formal project management context, this stage is an evaluation based on whether the criteria initially set up for the project has been met.

Moreover, DOI also details the adoption process from a consumer's point of view. So, the population of adopters is divided into five groups, which are distributed according to the time it takes them to adopt an innovation. They are: innovators (pioneers), early adopters (adventurous), early majority (deliberate), late majority (sceptical), and laggards (traditional) (Miles, 2012). These groups are directly correlated with an S-shaped curve, called the rate of adoption. This rate of adoption curve, in light blue, represents the cumulative of the bell-shaped curve of adopter categories, in dark blue, as it is shown in Figure 2.13.

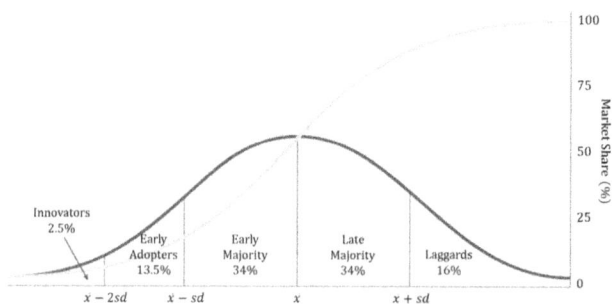

Figure 2.13: Rate of adoption curve and adopter groups. Source: Buchmann et al. (2021)

Additionally, the DOI theory explores the notion of key attributes inherent to innovations that can help in justifying innovations' adoption rates. These are characteristics that are generally valued by adopters and that should be considered by companies, when developing commercial

2.2 Technology Adoption in Organisations

strategies. These characteristics are, as defined by Rogers, the Five Attributes of Innovations (Rogers, 1995) (Greenhalgh et al., 2004):

- **Relative Advantage:** the degree to which an innovation is perceived as better than the product it's replacing, or competing products. Innovations that have a clear, unambiguous advantage in their effectiveness or cost-effectiveness are more easily adopted. If potential users see no relative advantage in the innovation they generally will not consider it any further. Relative advantage can be measured in quantitative aspects, such as cost or financial payback, but also in qualitative ones, like convenience or satisfaction. So, there are many sub-dimensions to relative advantage, such as the degree of economic profitability, low initial cost, a decrease in discomfort and immediacy of the reward. Relative Advantage is considered one of the best predictors of an innovation's rate of adoption, having a positive impact in it. Nevertheless, relative advantage alone does not guarantee widespread adoption.

- **Compatibility:** the degree to which an innovation is perceived to be consistent with the existing values, experience and needs of potential adopters. Incompatibility with values and norms of an individual or an organisation is a blocker when it comes to adoption of innovations. Familiarity with the innovation, due to past experiences, is an enabler for innovation adoption. In an organisational context, an innovation that fits with its existing values, norms, strategies, supporting technologies and ways of working is more likely to be adopted.

- **Complexity:** the degree to which an innovation is perceived as being difficult to understand or use. The more complex innovations generally take longer to be adopted, since the user has to acquire new skills and knowledge to use it.

- **Trialability:** the degree to which an innovation can be experimented with on a limited basis. This quality on an innovation makes it seem less uncertain to the user, making it more likely to get adopted, as long as the desirable effects of the innovation outweigh the undesirable ones.

- **Observability:** the degree to which the results of an innovation are visible to others. If potential adopters can see the benefits of a given innovation, before committing to it, they are more likely to adopt it. As potential adopters come to contact with existing users of an innovation, it spreads.

Empirical research supports the relevance of these attributes in the prediction of the adoption of innovations. For example, Brown et al. (2003) found that trialability and compatibility were major influences on cell phone banking adoption, and Oliveira et al. (2014) discovered that relative advantage and complexity have an influence in adoption of cloud computing in Portuguese firms.

In a separate analysis, Tornatzky and Klein (1982) identified other characteristics that affect technology adoption such as cost, communicability and social approval. The adoption of an innovation, however, also increases complexity at the management level of a company, and new aspects must be addressed, such as organisational structure, leadership's readiness to change, qualification and staff numbers, among others (Oliveira et al., 2014). As such, the DOI theory can be complemented by the Technology-Organization-Environment (TOE) framework, proposed by Tornatzky and Fleischer in 1990 Tornatzky et al. (1990).

2.2.2 The Technology-Organisation-Environment (TOE) Framework

The TOE framework explains the role of the technological, organisational and environmental contexts on technology adoption by organisations, aiming to account for concrete organisational factors in the decision to adopt innovation (Karunagaran et al., 2019).

2.2.2.1 Technology

The technological context refers to the relevance of the technology to the organisation, versus the alternatives available. Aside from the attributes of innovations proposed in the DOI theory, which are widely used in the technological context of the TOE framework, the degree of novelty of an innovation impacts the consumer's reaction to it, and consequent adoption. Relating to the degree of novelty, the two extreme ends are incremental and disruptive innovations. Incremental innovations are minor improvements or simple adjustments in current technology, thus the adoption of these kinds of shifts should be facilitated through contact with the external environment, where it's already being used (Munson and Pelz, 1979). At the pinnacle of novelty are disruptive innovations, which emerge in high-technology niche sectors that feature pioneering technology, and are initially perceived as unattractive to well-established companies, due to the change in status quo they represent (Christensen et al., 2013). In fact, additive manufacturing has been referred to as a disruptive innovation in several industries, including aerospace, biomedical and automotive (Martin et al., 2017) (Kok et al., 2018) (Rochus et al., 2007). Researchers have proposed differences between predictors of the adoption of disruptive and incremental innovations. For example, managerial attitude towards change and technical knowledge resources are expected to facilitate disruptive innovations, whereas structural complexity and decentralization should lead to incremental innovation (Dewar and Dutton, 1986) (Ettlie et al., 1984).

AM's use in the space sector is still relatively moderate, but it's seen rapid developments in the technologies and materials available (Sacco and Moon, 2019). The technology context determines which characteristics inherent to the innovation itself will constrain or facilitate the adoption of Additive Manufacturing.

2.2.2.2 Organisation

The Organisational context refers to the characteristics of the firm, such economic capacity, the organisational structure and resources, that have an impact on the strategy towards the adoption of technological innovations. Organisational characteristics may include the firm size, the degree of centralisation, the complexity of its managerial structure, and the amount monetary resources (Chau and Tam, 1997). In line with the monetary resources' is the adoption cost factor. Whether

2.2 Technology Adoption in Organisations

directly or indirectly, it greatly affects the acceptance and utilisation of any new technology. When an organisation decides whether or not to use a new technology, a cost-benefit analysis is almost always undertaken to determine its viability (Iacovou et al., 1995).

Although an organisation may be open to innovation in general, it may not be ready or prepared to adopt a specific invention. This concept is often referred to as Organisational Readiness. It is defined as "the availability of the needed organisational resources for adoption" (Iacovou et al., 1995). Characteristics that are associated with firms' readiness for adoption include support and advocacy, meaning that if supporters of an innovation outnumber and are more strategically located than opponents, the innovation is more likely to be adopted. Also, tracking the impact of an innovation increases the likelihood of it being deployed and maintained (Plsek, 2003) (Rogers, 1995) (Greenhalgh et al., 2004).

It is part of an organisations' decision strategy to partner with other organisations to create mutual benefits for both. This is a concept of Organisational Innovativeness. Organisations that maintain an innovation posture that positions them within the competitive market are more likely to adopt innovative technologies than the ones who don't (Ahmed et al., 2018).

2.2.2.3 Environment

The Environmental context entails market elements, competitors and the regulatory setting. These are factors external to an organisation that are constraints and opportunities for technological innovations to thrive (Tornatzky et al., 1990). Among these, market conditions, in terms of competitive market forces, and market uncertainty are major factors in the innovation process. Public entities', or governments', pressure and/or support can also influence the adoption of technological innovations. Governments can encourage the innovative process with supportive regulations and policies like financial incentives (Trang et al., 2016). In addition, with the growing need for sustainable and more environmentally conscious, governments are pressuring initiatives in line with these practices (Ford and Despeisse, 2016). For the space sector, the governmental institutions responsible for driving innovation in the field are Space Agencies, like ESA or NASA. Their main tasks are the proposal of Space Policies, that is, the definition of space programmes to be conducted within a certain time-frame and budgetary limits, that will then be submitted for approval to government authorities (Tugnoli and Wells, 2019). Furthermore, it's a space agency's job to ensure the implementation of the defined programmes, and they often act as their own research and development bodies to conduct research activities and testing of new technologies. The cooperation with private companies is an additional resource, when it's necessary to acquire specific technologies and systems. This type of contract has proved indispensable in many space activities in which the associated risks are high, and profit projections for a business to safely invest are uncertain. In the era of New Space, a shift is occurring, where now the risks and rewards are shared between public and private entities involved in a certain mission. A key aspect, however, of any partnership between public and private organisations is that the high-level requirements for spacecraft are defined by the Space Agency (Tugnoli and Wells, 2019).

Briefly, the study of technology adoption factors benefits from the combination of more than one theoretical model, for a better understanding of the phenomenon (Oliveira and Martins, 2011). The TOE framework makes Rogers's theory better able to explain organisational adoption of innovations (Chwelos et al., 2001). So, using both DOI and TOE theoretical perspectives provides an integrative research model, since the well-structured DOI theory lacks aspects which the TOE framework considers, particularly the Environment factor (Oliveira et al., 2014).

Chapter 3

Research Method

Technology adoption by organisations is a complex process that involves investment of time and resources. The lack of adoption of innovations is a prevalent problem noticed in the practise of organisational development and performance improvement. Often, an invention is developed and implemented, but it is not embraced by other portions of the organisation or by other organisations that would benefit from it (Lundblad, 2003). This is prevalent across industries, and the space one is no exception, especially considering that the space sector is living through a period of change (New Space), during which private companies now have access to space and can contribute to the development and testing of space technologies. This means that new participants might be interested in incorporating emerging technologies in their operations, including AM. Consequently, it is relevant to identify the main applications for this manufacturing technique, its benefits and drawbacks in the space context and general reasons for confidence and/or scepticism towards it. This study fills a research gap in the AM field, by not only evaluating its applicability in the space sector and current trends, but by analysing the factors that affect the adoption of it in space organisations.

This chapter is divided in four sections, to explain the different stages that compose the method used to accomplish this dissertation's goals.

3.1 Research Design

Considering that the adoption of additive manufacturing technologies in the space sector is not widely studied, an exploratory qualitative method was deemed as appropriate to address the theme. Qualitative exploratory studies are useful to address interpretive research questions, allowing for a deeper analysis of subject that's being studied (Leedy and Ormrod, 2019). Qualitative research is an approach for exploring and understanding the subjective perspectives of individuals or groups regarding an emerging phenomenon (Creswell and Creswell, 1994).

The TOE factors will be used as the basis for the interpretation of results. To adjust the TOE framework to the context of this book, the adoption factors were reviewed and adapetd. Specifically, the Technology factor of the TOE framework is composed by some of the DOI attributed of innovations. Complexity was not deemed as appropriate for this study, and was not considered. Figure 3.1 shows the adapted TOE framework, containing the factors that were used for results' analysis.

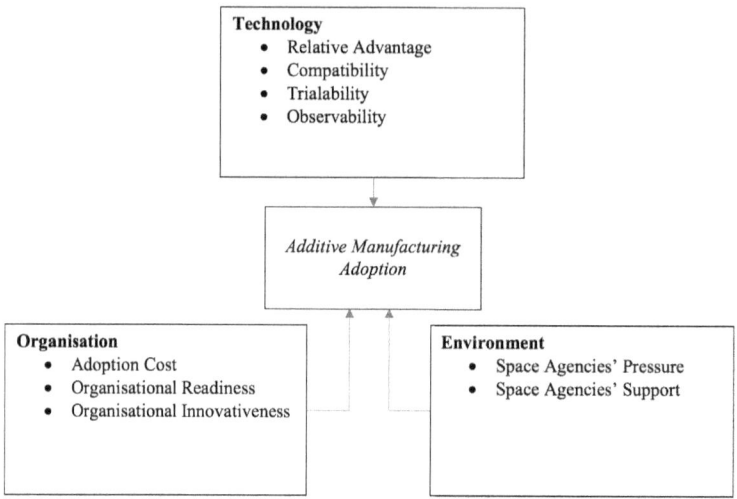

Figure 3.1: Adapted TOE Framework

The concepts of Government Pressure and Government Support, described in Section 2.2.2.3, translate to Space Agencies' Pressure and Support in the context of this book, since it's the space agencies' standards and guidelines that the organisations follow, and being the space agencies the main contributors to space activities in general. Being space agencies part of the public administration, this switch from Government to Space Agency is appropriate.

3.2 Data Collection

The data collection process for this book was made by conducting interviews with relevant entities in the space industry who are familiar with AM technologies. This method was chosen because having in-depth interviews with experts allows for a better understanding of the different perspectives about the subject, making the collected data more informative and accurate. Also, being this book an exploratory study about the adoption of AM in space organisations, it is clear that the inputs of actors in said space organisations are the most valuable. The use of highly knowledgeable informants who see the focal phenomenon from several angles is vital for the success of an interview-based study (Eisenhardt and Graebner, 2007). Maccoby and Maccoby (1954) defined the interview as "a (...) verbal exchange, in which one person, the interviewer, attempts to elicit information or expressions of opinion or belief from another person". Interviews

3.2 Data Collection

are divided into three groups: structured, un-structured and semi-structured. Structured interviews consist of administering questionnaires with fixed questions, in a standardised manner (Britten, 1995). On the other end of the spectrum are unstructured interviews. Even though no interview is fully devoid of structure, unstructured interviews are viewed as informal conversations, in which neither the questions' or answers' categories are predetermined, and rely solely on the interaction between researcher and informant (DiCicco-Bloom and Crabtree, 2006). In between these two groups are semi-structured interviews, which were the ones used in this study. Semi-structured interviews employ a mix of standard questions and individually tailored questions to elicit not only expected but also unexpected information from the interviewee (Leedy and Ormrod, 2019).

The present qualitative research has the objective of analysing the main adoption factors of AM in space organisations, which is quite a narrow and specific goal. Therefore, the sample of interviewees should be reasonably homogeneous and share similarities related to the research problem (McCracken, 1988). The decision process regarding the selection of participants was based on the need of knowledge and expertise in this under-explored topic. Thus, a loose technique called purposive sampling was used (Battaglia et al., 2008). Purposive Sampling is defined as the deliberate selection of participants based on their characteristics. It's a non-random strategy that relies on the researcher's judgement, considering what needs to be known and who is willing to supply the information, due to their knowledge or experience (Battaglia et al., 2008). It's commonly used in qualitative research to find and pick the most information-rich examples and make the most use of the available resources (Patton, 2002). This entails identifying people who are proficient and knowledgeable about the topic (Cresswell and Plano Clark, 2011).

For this study, the selection of most participants took place in a space technology event called "SpaceTech Expo Europe", that took place in Bremen, Germany in November 2021. This event is labelled as the supply-chain meeting place for the space industry, where the latest technological innovations for space manufacturing, components and systems for spacecraft are showcased. It hosts hundreds of companies that represent all sectors of the aerospace supply-chain. During the event, 21 companies were approached to discuss this topic and were later contacted and asked to participate in an interview. However, only 5 companies accepted this invite. After the SpaceTech Expo, the remaining participants were chosen based off general knowledge on the space sector, resulting in interviews with the European Space Agency, and the Additive Manufacturing sector, resulting in interviews with one expert in the matter. From these connections, an additional interview was scheduled. Table 3.1 displays the participants in this study, as well as the the organisations they're part of.

Table 3.1: Characteristics of the Interviewees and their corresponding Organisations

Interviewee	Education	Current Position in the Organisation	Field of Activity	Organisation Size
I1	MSc in Industrial Engineering	Sales Strategy and Operations Manager	3D Printing with composite materials	45
I2	BSc in Mechanical and Aeronautical Engineering	Head of Flight Hardware	Mechanical Ground Support Equipment for satellites	300
I3	MSc in Mechanical Engineering	Technology and Industrialisation Engineer	Mechanical Ground Support Equipment for satellites	300
I4	MSc in Industrial Engineering	Manager Defence and Space Technology	Composites parts, panels, laminates, and honeycomb core materials	86
I5	PhD in Production Engineering	Additive Manufacturing Coordinator	Space systems, Aerospace and Digital	812
I6	BSc in Mechanical Engineering and Minor in Entrepreneurism	Managing Director/Chief Executive Officer (CEO)	Industrial additive manufacturing for advanced applications using Aerospace-Grade Polymers	6
I7	MSc in Aerospace, Aeronautical and Astronautical Engineering	Chief Technology Officer (CTO)	Design, manufacture, and placement of nanosatellites to collect optical data	53
I8	BSc in Mechanical Engineering	Head of Innovation and Ventures Office	European Space Agency	2200
I9	PhD in Materials Processing	Advanced Manufacturing Engineer	European Space Agency	2200
I10	MSc in Mechanical Engineering	Technical Team Manager – Composite	Materials and Additive	408

3.2 Data Collection

Interviewees I1 to I7 belong to private companies that develop solutions for space applications and/or work with AM technologies. I2 and I3 belong to the same company, and were both present in the same interview, with separate insights. Interviewees I8 and I9 work for the European Space Agency, an international organisation with 18 Member States, which is responsible for developing the European Space program, ensuring that investment in space delivers benefits to European citizens. Both are knowledgeable in AM and how it fits in the space sector. Finally, I10 works for a research organisation, with focus in material science, and is an expert in AM, particularly for the space sector.

As previously mentioned, semi-structured interviews were chosen for this study and three scripts were produced beforehand, one for the private companies' participants, another for ESA's participants and a final one for I10. Considering the nature of semi-structured interviews, the scripts were used as the main guide for the interviews and, when necessary, complementary questions were asked throughout, according to the topic of the conversation and the answers of the interviewees. The scripts are attached to this document in Appendixes A, B and C. Due to the various and distant locations of all participants, the interviews were conducted via video-call. They were recorded, with consent from the participants, to facilitate the note-taking and transcribing processes required for retrieving relevant results. The average duration of these calls was 30 minutes, resulting in a total of 5 hours of data to examine. All interviews were led in English, except for one, with interviewee I10, which was conducted in Portuguese.

All participants are aware and knowledgeable of AM. They are cognisant of the existing technologies, materials and potential applications, which provides grounds for valid results in terms of why or why not they decided to pursue it, and for what. Table 3.2 details the participants' position regarding the adoption of additive manufacturing, based on Rogers' stages of adoption, discussed in Section 2.2.1. Among the interviewees are people who were considered to be in pre-adoption stages of innovation, since they are part of organisations that develop new technology, but don't apply/commercialise it. They are I8, I9 and I10 and are identified as N/A in Table 3.2.

Table 3.2: Interviewees and their Organisations' AM Adoption Stage

Interviewee	Organisation	Adoption Stage
I1	Private Company	5. Confirmation
I2, I3	Private Company	3. Decision
I4	Private Company	2. Persuasion
I5	Private Company	4. Implementation
I6	Private Company	5. Confirmation
I7	Private Company	2. Persuasion
I8, I9	ESA	N/A
I10	Research Organisation	N/A

3.3 Data Analysis

The data analysis process began with the transcription of the audio files that resulted from recording the interviews to text. This was the first step where a data analysis software, MAXQDA, was used. MAXQDA is a software for qualitative and mixed methods data analysis. The choice for this software resided on the fact that it allows the user to create categories and sub-categories and attributing them to certain excerpts from the transcription.

Categorisation is a procedure for classifying constructive elements from a set by differentiating them. Classifying elements into categories implies knowing what they have in common with one another. The primary goal of categorisation is to provide a simplified representation of raw data (Bardin, 2013). In this study, the categorisation was done using the content analysis method. Berelson (1952) defined content analysis as "a research technique for the objective, systematic and quantitative description of the manifest content of communication". This definition, however, doesn't entail both quantitative and qualitative research methods so, a new one was proposed by Krippendorff (2018): "content analysis as a research method is a systematic and objective means of describing and quantifying phenomena, also known as a method for analysing documents". Through content analysis, it is possible to distil words into fewer content-related categories. It is assumed that when words and phrases are placed in the same categories, they share the same meaning (Cavanagh, 1997). It is imperative that in this passage from raw to organised data there is no deviations in material, by excess or default.

Generically, good categories are mutually exclusive, homogeneous, pertinent and objective (Bardin, 2013). In this study, the categories were constructed in MAXQDA to facilitate the analysis of the transcripts and provide answers to the research objectives, while also considering the TOE framework created for this study. To understand how AM is being used in the space industry, a category called "Additive Manufacturing" was created. Some subcategories aren't related to factors that affect the adoption of AM in organisations and, as such, aren't fitted in the TOE Framework, and are labelled as "N/A". Aiming to understand the main reasons why, or why not, 3D printing is an interesting and appealing innovation for space-related applications, two categories were created: Drivers and Barriers. Each of these has multiple subcategories, mainly regarding technological features which make AM suitable, or not, for space and other aspects regarding general advantages and disadvantages. Table 3.3 shows the categories that were used for data analysis, and how they fit into the adapted TOE framework.

Table 3.3: Categories of Analysis

Categories	Subcategories	TOE Framework
Additive Manufacturing	Applications	N/A
	Materials	N/A
	Design Methods	N/A
	Opportunities	N/A
Drivers	Integration	Organisation
	Cost	Organisation
	Customisation	Technology
	Complexity/Design Freedom	Technology
	Weight Reduction	Technology
	Lead Times	Environment
	Reliability	Technology
Barriers	Certification	Environment
	Final Part Quality	Technology
	Repeatability	Technology
	Certification	Environment
	Availability of Resources	Technology
	Knowledge/Skills	Organisation

Chapter 4

Results

The analysis of results will be presented throughout four sections. Initially, the opportunities in the field that interviewees considered relevant will be discussed as well as current trends in materials and technologies for 3D printing. After that, three subsections represent each context from the TOE framework: **Technology**, where the factors of the DOI theory relevant in the context of this study that affect its adoption in space companies are reviewed; **Organisation**, where internal aspects or the organisation's strategy that impact adoption are presented and **Environment**, where external aspects are analysed.

4.1 Opportunities for AM in the Space Sector

From the interviews, it was possible to gain awareness of the fields within the space sector that AM can be useful in. Although these trends and opportunities aren't necessarily factors that affect adoption at an organisational level, they are relevant in the theme of this book, and contribute to literature on the topics of AM in the space industry setting.

All interviewees mentioned the materials their organisations are using and/or are considering using in their activities with 3D printing. The results reveal that, for space applications, metallic materials are still the first choice, since they provide great mechanical properties and perform well in the space environment. The fact that metallic materials don't exhibit outgassing was mentioned as an advantage for space use. For the structure of satellites, aluminium and its alloys are preferred due to their low densities. Titanium and its alloys, namely Ti-6Al-4V, are used when temperature requirements are higher. For propulsion systems, nickel alloys and precious metals are used, and copper is also a trend in this field. For printing parts with metals, PBF and DED technologies are the main ones used. PBF is appropriate for small parts with high accuracy, although surface treatment is often required afterwards to improve surface quality, since some roughness can be verified immediately after printing. For example, PBF is used for brackets, like the ones in Figure 2.6 and for lattice structures, like the one shown in Figure 4.1. Lattice structures offer a way to reduce mass and cost for several parts such as nozzles. For bigger parts with less strict requirements in terms of accuracy, DED technologies are used. The process is faster than PBF, but the final parts always need to be machined afterwards, since the surface quality is generally not good.

Figure 4.1: Latticed engine nozzle. Source: ESA (2014)

Even though metals still hold their place as the most reliable materials for space applications, the participants recognise the recent developments in polymers for space. Also, it was referred that CubeSats are a great way to experiment with new materials, namely polymers. PEEK and Polyetherketoneketone (PEKK) are the main ones used for space applications. However, as far as 3D printing goes, these materials are also the hardest to print, due to their fusion temperature, high viscosity, and crystallinity. It's also difficult to print large structures using them, because the printing equipment gets worn out. An alternative to PEEK and PEKK is Polyethylenimine (PEI), because its fusion temperature is lower, and hence they're easier to print.

AM with composite materials for space applications is still in a very early development stage, and there aren't any final parts that have flown using composites, according to I7 and I8. They require careful attention in the printing process since the fibres are quite abrasive and can be harmful to the nozzle of the printer. One area where composites are promising is lattice structures, used for panels in satellites. 3D printing allows for the manufacture of complex designs, such as lattice structures, and proves to be suitable for this application, according to I4.

Even though there have been developments in the materials' aspect of 3D printing, some participants still consider that finding materials suitable for both space applications and 3D printing is a barrier to the diffusion of this innovation. As mentioned by I10, the materials that are most interesting for space applications, are also the ones which are more difficult to print.

Regarding opportunities for AM, a trend that I8 and I9 mentioned was in-space manufacturing. This is applied to two main areas: the **manufacturing of small objects**, like tools, spare parts and medical devices and for astronauts in orbit, and the **manufacturing of big structures**. For the first application, it is predictable that polymers are the main materials that will be used. The latter, which is still in an early stage of development, is focused on building "factory-like" structure in space, namely in Mars. Here, all supplies needed would be additively manufactured using, among other materials, planetary regolith.

Aside from in-space manufacturing, interviews with members of private companies revealed that some existing fields could use improvements, like composite additive manufacturing and the introduction of multiple functions into one part (thermal, structural, etc.). Also, all additively manufactured parts that have flown to space were secondary structures, so, another opportunity for AM in the industry is the manufacturing of primary structures to fly. Besides, with the improvement of processes and the increasingly better surface finishing, it will be possible further incorporate AM in the production of final parts, according to I10. Regarding the way AM works, that is, layer by layer deposition of material, in the z-axis, I10 predicts that free-form AM is the ultimate goal. Free-form AM refers to the manufacturing of parts from all orientations, and not just from the bottom to the top.

4.2 Technology

On the technological context, and relating back to Figure 3.1, the factors that will be examined in the results are the ones described in the DOI theory, and that are relevant in the present study: Relative Advantage, Compatibility, Trialability and Observability.

4.2.1 Relative Advantage

In this study, Relative Advantage was conceptualised as the reason that leads organisations to use AM for space applications, as opposed to conventional manufacturing processes. As mentioned in Subsection 2.1.2, relative advantage is one of the main factors that affects adoption, meaning that if organisations view AM technologies as better for their activitiy than conventional techniques, they are more likely to adopt it. The aspects that were most mentioned by participants as advantageous in comparison with conventional manufacturing processes were the **freedom of design** AM allows for and the **mass reduction** aspect.

Regarding freedom of design, that is, the possibility to create objects with complex geometries, otherwise impossible to manufacture using conventional methods, most participants (I2, I3, I4, I5, I6, I7, I8, I9, I10) consider it a unique advantage of AM technologies. As I6 points out, it's possible to "add a lot of complexity to the designs, without increasing costs". Interviewees consider this feature the true strength of AM: the possibility of creating new and complex parts, that fit exactly the structural requirements of the application. In line with this aspect, is the topology optimisation method, discussed in Section 2.2.1, which is mentioned by 4 participants (I5, I6, I8 and I9). They consider it to have ground-breaking potential for AM, especially for metals, where it is crucial to reduce material usage, due to their higher density. With TO, it is possible to design a part for manufacturing in a way that material is placed solely where it is required, that is, where the loads are. This minimises material usage and, consequently, mass.

The mass reduction aspect, in the scope of AM, refers to the fact that with AM there are virtually no restrictions when it comes to geometry, and it's possible to use less material, obtaining the same results, regarding performance. Also, since AM produces parts layer by layer, they can be manufactured with less joints and connecting elements, thus reducing mass as well. The participants who point mass reduction as an advantage are I2, I3, I5, I6, I8, I9 and I10. Out of these, I2, I3, I5 and I6 belong to organisations in a later stage of adoption of AM, and I8, I9 and I10 are considered technology developers. I8 revealed that ESA's initial studies for AM were to specifically explore the advantage of mass reduction. It is considered that for satellites, even if the mass saving is of just a few grams, it's valid and important. In fact, I9 mentioned that the cost of sending 1kg to space can reach a cost of 40 000€.

The two aspects described above were the most mentioned, but not the only ones. A few participants (I1, I4 and I10) expressed concerns regarding the final part quality, both in terms of surface finishing and mechanical properties obtained, as being an issue of 3D printing.

Two interviewees haven't yet adopted AM in their production (I4 and I7), but both envision doing so in the future, since they perceive AM's advantages as beneficial for their activities. In fact, the reasons why they haven't used it yet are related to logistical and project-related issues, rather than technology-related.

4.2.2 Compatibility

The compatibility aspect of AM relates to how it suits the organisations' activities. Companies won't implement a new technological innovation unless it's compatible with their existing lines of business. I7 refers that the simplifying of operations, and accordingly, the supply chain are factors that are appealing to the company. The organisation has policies of keeping production locally, working with nearby suppliers and manufacturing in-house. So, I7 considers that 3D printing would help simplify the company's operations.

The integration of 3D printing is also related to the projects a company has in hands at a given point. I4 and I5 admitted that the use of AM, or any other manufacturing method, is solely related to the projects that the company is working for.

4.2.3 Trialability

Trialability is conceptualised as the importance of the experimentation phase a company goes through before the final decision of adopting an innovation. Some of the participants that were interviewed are part of organisations in early stages of adoption of AM (I2, I3, I4 and I7). It was found that experimenting with AM is part of these organisations' strategies to implement this innovation. The main uses foreseen in this initial phase for 3D printing are prototyping and modelling of test structure and test set-ups, but in a later stage for full production models, like some metal parts of the structure.

4.2.4 Observability

In the scope of this book, the definition of Observability overlaps with Rogers' presented in Section 2.2.1. That is, the degree to which the use of AM by space companies influences other space companies to do the same. In that sense, I6 considers observability an important aspect for AM adoption. Currently, there's lack of experience, and lack of significant data regarding materials for space applications and simultaneously adequate for 3D printing, hence, companies are reluctant to use it. However, in the future (5-10 years), as the process becomes more ubiquitous, it's likely to be more widely used, as I6 referred, "once all other companies are using it, the ones that aren't will change their minds".

4.3 Organisation

In the organisation context of the TOE Framework, the factors that will be discussed are Adoption Cost, Organisational Readiness and Organisational Innovativeness.

4.3.1 Adoption Cost

The process of organisational innovation is mainly shaped by costs and benefits. The Adoption Cost factor was described as the main factor organisations consider for the adoption of any new technological innovation. The participants who mentioned it referred that the decision always comes down to costs. In fact, I7 mentioned that the search for new technologies to implement in the organisation is based on "trying to reduce infrastructure costs, wherever it's possible" and I1 responds, when asked a question about the main drivers for adopting 3D printing "Cost reduction is the main reason behind the adoption of any new technology". Evidently, all other aspects are related to cost, like mass reduction, availability of materials/processes and qualification of parts.

Mostly, private companies' participants mention that the cost of producing 3D printed parts is still high, because the volume of production is low and the investment required for the equipment is high. This is a problem of repeatability, that has consequences in costs. If AM was suitable for mass production, the initial investment would be absorbed by the high production volume. However, according to I2 and I3, the parts produced in large volumes are generally not very complex and, therefore, wouldn't benefit from the advantages of 3D printing. This is corroborated by I10, which points out that not all parts benefit from the use of 3D printing, thus, a full transition from conventional methods to 3D printing isn't necessary or advantageous for organisations. For example, simple plaques or vats are components that wouldn't benefit from AM, while small components, like brackets found in satellites and nanosatellites are suitable for it. It's in this process of differentiating where to apply AM and where not to, that organisations focus their research efforts and where design optimisation techniques play an important role, once again.

As for positive aspects of AM with regards to costs, it is evident that less material usage leads to lower material costs. Also, the more lightweight a satellite structure is, the more payload it can carry, which is beneficial for companies sending satellites to space as well.

4.3.2 Organisational Readiness

Organisational Readiness relates to the internal aspects of the organisational structure that are hindering or prompting an innovation to be adopted across all sectors of the organisation. In this study, it refers to the knowledge and skills required to work with AM, and how this affects adoption.

The lack of knowledge and skills, both from higher positions and plant workers, was mentioned by 50% of participants (I1, I6, I7, I8 and I9). Relating to the TOE framework, this is an issue of organisational readiness. Participants claim that lack of knowledge and aversion to risk are big barriers to the spread of this innovation. I1 considers educating workers as a big part of the job, and that adopting new technologies is a long process. To facilitate this process, technology transfer must happen, that is, experts in AM must educate manufacturers how to use it and for which applications. According to I9, this process is very important, and innovation in companies is crucial to ensure their relevance and competitive advantage.

4.3.3 Organisational Innovativeness

One organisational aspect that was interesting to explore in the scope of this study was how private companies look for new technologies with potential benefits for their activities, which is the definition of Organisational Innovativeness. Partnerships with universities and research centres are organisational factors, since it's an organisations' internal decision to associate itself with universities to integrate innovative technologies in the productive processes, or if all research will be done in-house. All 6 participants who work in private companies and commercialise products have internal Research and Development (R&D) departments which oversee developing and testing new technologies. Out of these, 4 participants (I1, I5, I6 and I7) admitted having ties with universities, for research and technology integration purposes. In fact, the company I1 works for a company that was created as a result of a PhD book, and the contact between the company and the university remains. Also, I5 mentioned that, specifically for AM, the company worked with academic partners and research institutes to do the design, verification, and testing steps.

4.4 Environment

The Environmental factor of the TOE framework is related to external aspects that influence an organisation's adoption process of innovations. In this book, the relevant aspects to consider were the Space Agencies' Pressure and Support.

4.4.1 Space Agencies' Support

All participants admit following ESA's platforms, as a way to bring innovativeness to their organisations. ESA has a number of opportunities for firms and research institutes to present proposals for new R&D products and technologies, which are included in Calls for Proposal. Additionally, I8, I9 and I10 mentioned the Open Space Innovation Platform (OSIP), an online

4.4 Environment

platform created by ESA in 2019, being the main entry point for novel ideas into ESA. Anyone interested in contributing to European space research and interact with space industry experts can submit ideas in the platform. Also, I10 mentioned having attended an ESA event, where companies in the sector shared ideas, business opportunities and trending research topics.

4.4.2 Space Agencies' Pressure

In the era of New Space, most Space Agencies are adapting their strategies and ways of interacting with the private sector to match and foster the emergence of private endeavours, building new types of partnerships and readjusting their role. The role of space agencies is changing from one of orchestrating/directing role, to a more facilitating one driven by commercialisation needs. As such, Space Agencies' Pressure was defined as the difficulties felt by private companies in terms of certification and compliance with space sector requirements for Additive Manufacturing of parts for space. It is important to note that the Space Agencies' roles aren't of overseeing companies' activities and developments, but rather one of cooperating and providing knowledge. It's part of a Space Agencies' role, in its R&D activities to develop standards and requirements for parts to go to space, and that private organisations should consider.

A big part of the space industry which makes it unique, is the very specific requirements that are involved in it. This is heavily felt by the participants who work in private companies, and directly with AM (I1, I2, I3, I5, I6). As put by I2, "qualifying a part made with 3D printing is very expensive and time-consuming". Currently, the company I2 and I3 belong to uses 3D printing only for tooling purposes, and the participants don't see it as a main activity for the company in the nearing future. They add that the ESA standard to have many limitations regarding what is possible to do with 3D printing, and view AM as something that should be avoided, unless it's specifically requested from a client. Alongside these participants, also I8 and I9 mention this factor as a barrier for adopting AM. As mentioned by I9, "what's stopping the adoption of AM as a routine manufacturing method is the intense certification it needs, and the high cost this represents".

3D printing is a special and difficult technological innovation in terms of certification because it's unpredictable and stochastic in a way that parts made with the exact same process may turn out different from each other, in terms of internal structures and defects. To manufacture any part, it's important to ensure that the material is right, as well as the machine settings and the design. This makes the process of certification and validation extremely costly and time-consuming for companies, which may have to test each part individually.

Chapter 5 Discussion

Chapter 5

Discussion

From an early stage in this investigation, it was possible to perceive that the use of 3D printing for space is in the initial phase of adoption, but most participants appear optimistic and invested in its potential. Out of all participants, only I2 and I3, which belong to the same company, have a sceptical attitude towards using it for now, as they've had problems with AM in the past. Even so, the potential for this manufacturing process is recognised, and once the issues associated with it, particularly for the space industry, are resolved, there is aperture to integrating this innovation in their activities.

Regarding technical AM aspects, such as materials, technologies and opportunities in the sector, the results corroborated the literature review. As referred in Section 2.1.1, the materials of choice for space applications are metals, namely aluminium and titanium alloys. Naturally, the developments of AM for manufacturing space components are mainly focused on metals and the technologies suited for them, PBF and DED. Metallic components have flown to space, like the one in Figure 2.6, and many others are reported in literature. Metal AM, that is, mainly PBF and DED technologies, are considered as validated for space use and ESA has issued a standard with requirements and recommendations for PBF technologies. Regarding polymers, their use for satellite components, and structures is mostly experimental, but they exhibit potential for small satellites, like the one in Figure 2.7 and, more importantly, for in-space manufacturing of spare parts and tools. Although PEEK has relevant properties for the space environment, making it appealing for structure manufacturing, its printing process still has limitations. As such, PEI could be a better alternative, since its mechanical properties make it more suitable for 3D printing. Finally, additive manufacturing using composites is emerging field with room for improvements, and no final part using both AM and composites has been sent to space.

The TOE Framework, which served as a theoretical framework for this book, hasn't been used in the scope of Additive Manufacturing Technologies for Space Applications. As such, this study provides preliminary data on this subject. Table 5.1 shows which factors of the TOE framework were mentioned by participants, evidencing the most relevant ones.

Table 5.1: TOE Framework Factors mentioned by Interviewees

	I1	I2	I3	I4	I5	I6	I7	I8	I9	I10
Relative Advantage	✓	✓	✓	✓	✓	✓	✓	✓	✓	✓
Compatiblity				✓	✓		✓			
Trialibility				✓			✓			
Observability						✓				
Adoption Cost	✓				✓	✓		✓		
O. Readiness	✓					✓	✓	✓	✓	
O. Innovativeness	✓				✓	✓	✓			
S.A. Pressure	✓	✓	✓		✓	✓		✓	✓	
S.A. Support	✓	✓	✓	✓	✓	✓	✓	✓	✓	✓

The most relevant factors mentioned during the interviews, and which justify further analysis are Relative Advantage, Adoption Cost, Organisational Readiness, and Space Agencies' Pressure. Even though the Space Agencies' Support factor was mentioned by all participants, it will not be further explored in this section. The relationship between the companies and the Space Agencies is clear and was explained in Section 4.4.1, and thus, it doesn't require further explanation and discussion.

The **Relative Advantage** factor focused on two strands, the freedom of design and the mass reduction, both features that AM offers and are beneficial to the space sector. As previously mentioned, AM's potential in the space sector lies in the fabrication of complex parts that are either cost-prohibitive or, in some cases, impossible to fabricate using conventional manufacturing methods. An important remark on the freedom of design factor is that using AM to manufacture objects that are conventionally manufactured isn't always beneficial and, as such, it's key to analyse which geometries benefit from AM and which don't, in order to reach this technology's full potential. Along with utilising the potential of AM in terms of producing objects, it's important to make use of techniques such as topology optimisation, to fully adapt production to this method. Thus, the advantage of the freedom of design of AM comparing to other methods is a fact that participants agree on. On the other hand, the mass reduction strand is not as straightforward. While participants agree that reducing the mass of space components is crucial in manufacturing for space, I2 and I3 consider that necessary effort for using additive manufacturing in their operations isn't worth the mass reduction it gets. Furthermore, and particularly for small satellites, I7 (which is part of a recent company that isn't widely experienced in AM) considers that the mass aspect isn't important, since these satellites are already small and lightweight. When considering small satellites for commercial applications, they're part of a constellation of satellites, composed of up to 150 units. As such, the mass reduction aspect shouldn't refer to one small satellite, which is, indeed, already lightweight, but rather to the whole constellation, where mass savings in each unit make up for large and significant weight savings in the constellation as a whole. Contrarily, the remaining participants, especially I8, I9 and I10 view mass reduction as an ever-present priority for space components, even if the weight savings are small, of just a few grams.

The **Adoption Cost** is a at the forefront of organisation's decision to adopt any innovation, even though not all participants mentioned it explicitly. All other factors are directly or indirectly related to cost, being the reduction in material usage the most seemingly obvious AM feature that contributes to cost reduction. Furthermore, assembly cost is minimised as parts can be produced in one sitting. Lead times are also reduced, as parts can be manufactured immediately after the design process; and using additively manufactured components, which are generally lightweight, can reduce energy consumption and, consequently, costs (Ford and Despeisse, 2016). Being AM an ideal process for customised and low-volume manufacturing, it's suitable for occasions where producing a single component is costly-prohibitive, but necessary in industrial settings. One example is the production of spare parts, highly applicable to the space sector. With the intention of further reducing costs, which are already steep in the space industry, and extending product life-cycle, material recycling represents a promising opportunity in the sector. As AM is still in an early stage of adoption, it leaves room for developing technologies to extend the objects' life-cycles. The literature shows that this is a trending field, and yet another reason for organisations to consider adopting AM (Ford and Despeisse, 2016).

Organisational Readiness was mentioned by 5 participants. There is an organisational lack of knowledge surrounding 3D printing, despite the amount of information on the topic that is readily available. Participants referred that this issue is present across all organisational levels, starting from engineers, who may feel distrust towards AM and its capabilities of producing high-performing parts, just like conventional manufacturing methods. This issue affects production workers as well, who don't receive proper training on how to utilise the machines to their full potential. The managerial attitude towards change is a factor with great influence on the adoption of emerging technologies, but, with regards to disruptive innovations, it's common that doubts and mistrust occur. Solving the issue of lack of organisational readiness regarding new technology adoption may involve an evaluation phase, where readiness is "measured", with regards to process, people, work environment and IT infrastructure. This first phase happens before implementation, and represents an early warning about the risks tied with an innovation, thus acting as a buffer towards them. It also allows organisations to estimate the required level of organisational change in order to implement a new technological innovation (Alshawi, 2007).

The **Space Agencies' Pressure** was directly linked with the subcategory of data analysis "Certification". This factor was mentioned by all participants except for those that are in phase 2 of the adoption process, and that haven't used AM to produce final parts yet. Upon further investigation, it was possible to comprehend how the certification of parts for spaceflight occurs and why is it a barrier in adopting AM. The need for qualification and certification of parts comes from the fact that these missions are extremely costly in resources and time, and it's imperative to ensure that the spacecraft will not fail. It's in both the Space Agency's and the company's (in case of collaboration) best interest to comply with space requirements developed by Space Agencies, as part of their R&D activities. According to a NASA Technical Memorandum, the path to qualification and verification of parts made by AM is a universal concern echoed throughout government, industry, and academia. Industry adoption of parts made by AM is slow because of ambiguity in current validation and verification approaches. For AM, the qualification process to certify parts in terms of unity, efficacy, and applicability, is especially complicated due to the variety of machine types and technologies available. Another difficulty regarding qualification has to do with testing of parts made by AM, since there is a clear lack of defined critical defect types and sizes, as well as reference standards. Also, the use of in-process monitoring techniques isn't yet common, which means that parts must be inspected individually, slowing down the productive process. In-process monitoring of the part during the building process may be a game changer in improving the consistency, repeatability, and uniformity across machines, which in turn will facilitate the qualification and certification of the part (Waller et al., 2014).

Chapter 6

Conclusion

Additive Manufacturing is becoming a viable method for the manufacturing of final parts, expanding its initial applications of rapid prototyping and tooling. The space sector is one that's on the forefront of this paradigm shift, mainly benefiting from AM's possibility to manufacture any object, without the design constraints imposed by conventional manufacturing methods (Huang et al., 2015).

This study was an early attempt to explore and develop an AM adoption model, that was theoretically grounded in the TOE framework. This book was prompted by the NewSat project, which aims to develop and ground test a nanosatellite, using AM technologies. Particularly, the task in hands for the project was to review the state-of-the-art of practices and international collaboration efforts regarding the adoption of emerging technologies in space research. Relating back to the research questions proposed in Section 1.3, it was possible to draw conclusions regarding the main **technological benefits of AM**, the **applications of AM technologies in the space sector** and, finally, **the factors that affect an organisation's decision to adopt AM**.

Firstly, AM makes it possible to manufacture highly complex structures, for example, latticed structures, which are often necessary in the sector. Additionally, the possibility of producing geometrically complex structures prompts the re-imagining of the design process as well. With methods like topology optimisation, it's possible to create optimised structures using less material, thus reducing weight, while maintaining structural performance. This is especially important in the space industry, where weight savings are always a priority. As such, it's important to not only use AM as a manufacturing method, and using it for all parts that were once made with conventional methods, but also to adapt the design to AM.

Regarding the applications of AM in the space sector, components for spacecraft, like brackets, nozzles and other secondary components are the main uses for AM technologies, currently. Also, AM is being researched and starting to be used for producing spare parts and tools in-orbit as they're needed, and for small satellite structures. Lastly, two emerging but very promising fields for AM are the manufacturing of big structures in-space, using planetary soil, and the manufacturing of objects with multiple functions.

As for the factors which affect an organisation's decision to adopt AM, it was found that all contexts from the TOE framework have an influence on a doption: Technology, Organisation and Environment. Within these contexts, the factors which have the most significant impact are **Relative Advantage**, in the form of technological benefits of AM, comparing to conventional manufacturing methods; **Adoption Cost**, a crucial factor considered in all organisational decisions; **Organisational Readiness**, that is, the knowledge of the technologies, materials, and potential of AM, across hierarchical levels; and finally, **Space Agencies' Pressure**, as validating parts for spaceflight is a costly and time-consuming process, which companies often don't see as beneficial to their business.

In addition, an interesting remark is that, despite all the important achievements of the New Space era, companies still rely on and maintain strong bonds with space agencies. It's possible to infer that this bond between the private and public space sectors is beneficial for both parts, as companies gain expertise and innovative insights by participating in conferences and events, or even funding and support with research activities.

Finally, regarding the transition of AM as a method used solely for prototyping to a method used for the production of final parts. The requirements for a prototype are inferior to those of a final part, and, through the interviews, it was possible to note that the AM process hasn't evolved in order to meet the stricter requirements of final part manufacturing. That is, this process doesn't ensure the repeatability and quality necessary in order to make it a routine method for final part maufacturing.

6.1 Future Work

Given the early stage of adoption of AM in space organisations, a qualitative approach was deemed appropriate, to gain better understanding of the problem and obtain more in-depth data regarding the underlying factors that influence adoption of AM in space organisations. Following this work, the first step would be to expand the number of interviews, mainly with companies in different stages of adoption of AM, and with other Space Agencies. Also, all companies which were represented in this study are European, and work in collaboration with ESA, thus, it would be interesting to inquire participants from other continents, working with major space organisations. Additionally, this book provides grounds for the development of a technological roadmap and detailed guide for the adoption of Additive Manufacturing Technologies for space organisations.

www.ingramcontent.com/pod-product-compliance
Lightning Source LLC
LaVergne TN
LVHW020443080526
838202LV00055B/5327